the empathetic sketchbook
a 30 day project guide

the empathetic sketchbook

a 30 day project guide

– liza rein

beat up bear publishing 2018

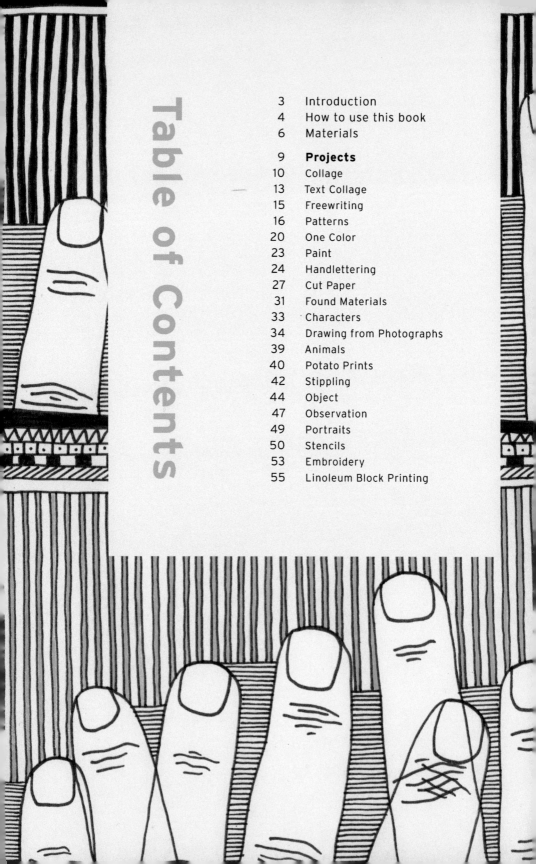

Table of Contents

3   Introduction
4   How to use this book
6   Materials

9   **Projects**
10 Collage
13 Text Collage
15 Freewriting
16 Patterns
20 One Color
23 Paint
24 Handlettering
27 Cut Paper
31 Found Materials
33 Characters
34 Drawing from Photographs
39 Animals
40 Potato Prints
42 Stippling
44 Object
47 Observation
49 Portraits
50 Stencils
53 Embroidery
55 Linoleum Block Printing

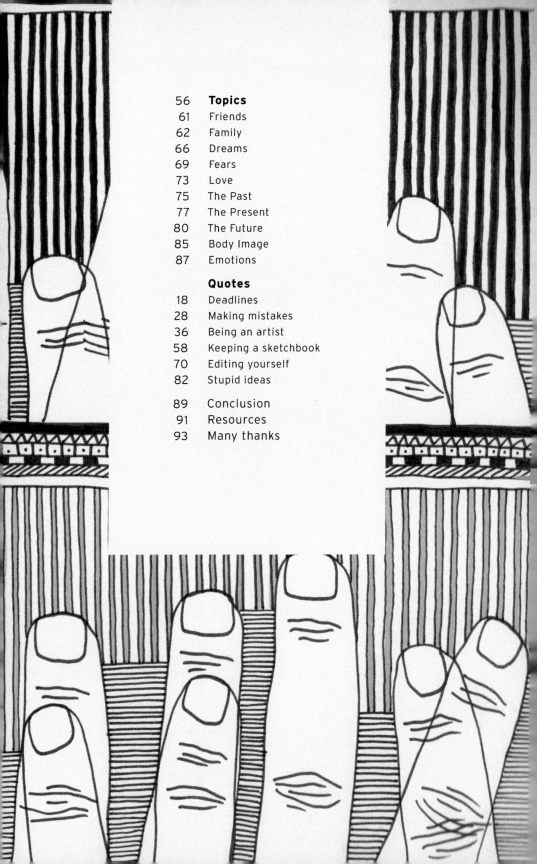

56 **Topics**
61 Friends
62 Family
66 Dreams
69 Fears
73 Love
75 The Past
77 The Present
80 The Future
85 Body Image
87 Emotions

Quotes
18 Deadlines
28 Making mistakes
36 Being an artist
58 Keeping a sketchbook
70 Editing yourself
82 Stupid ideas

89 Conclusion
91 Resources
93 Many thanks

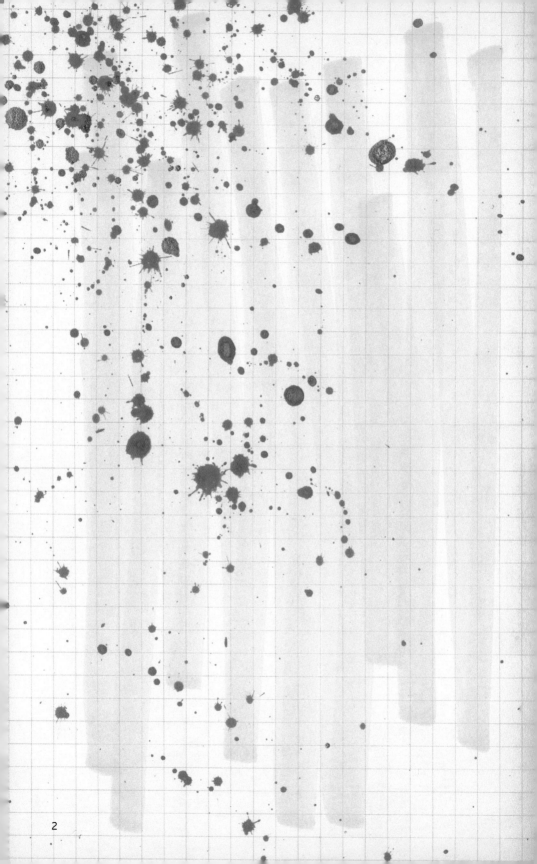

Middle school was a rough time for me. I was not really prepared for the transitions that I had to go through. Nor did I have any outlet for the isolation, depression and anger that I experienced during that time. Crying alone in my room, I didn't have any other way to vent these emotions. After making some new friends, I started finding ways to try to deal with my overwhelming reality. Unfortunately, besides passing five page notes in class, these new coping techniques were not healthy for me.

When I first started to keep a sketchbook in high school, it was a revelation. I wrote endlessly about my day, friends, family, and school. It became a kind of diary with movie tickets and magazine clippings. Doodling in class became a ritual. Without the limits of lines in a spiral notebook, my blank sketchbook pages became a canvas for me to express whatever was in my head.

This was long before tumblr, art school and seeing the many types of sketchbooks that different artists keep. My sketchbooks were almost always in pen and marker. I would draw an alien with a bowling ball and light bulbs hanging from the top of the page all the time. But it wasn't what I drew that was important, it was that I had started to move away from internalizing my emotions and letting them out on paper.

With this guidebook, I hope to teach people that your sketchbook can be a problem solving tool, a place to vent, or rejoice. It will be a companion and a friend. It is a place to make mistakes, to glory in them, and to let go. Your sketchbook will be there for you when you're up, when you're down and everything in between.

How To Use
This Book

Empathetic Sketchbook outlines 30 projects
intended to be done in 30 days. The deadline
is intended to help you get through the projects
quickly and to complete a full sketchbook. This book
is intended to be a guide to help you explore
different techniques and to push you creatively
by giving you restrictions. Ultimately this book is
a guide and it's up to you to get creative and
experiment and have fun.

Projects 1–20 show a variety of different methods
that can be used in a sketchbook. They are intended
to be done frequently to get used to looking at your
sketchbook and materials in a new way.

Once you have explored these different methods,
projects 21–30 will ask you to explore different topics
such as family, emotions, your future and
your dreams. The topics are meant to stimulate
thought and emotional expression. There are
no rules, no boundaries: the sky is the limit!

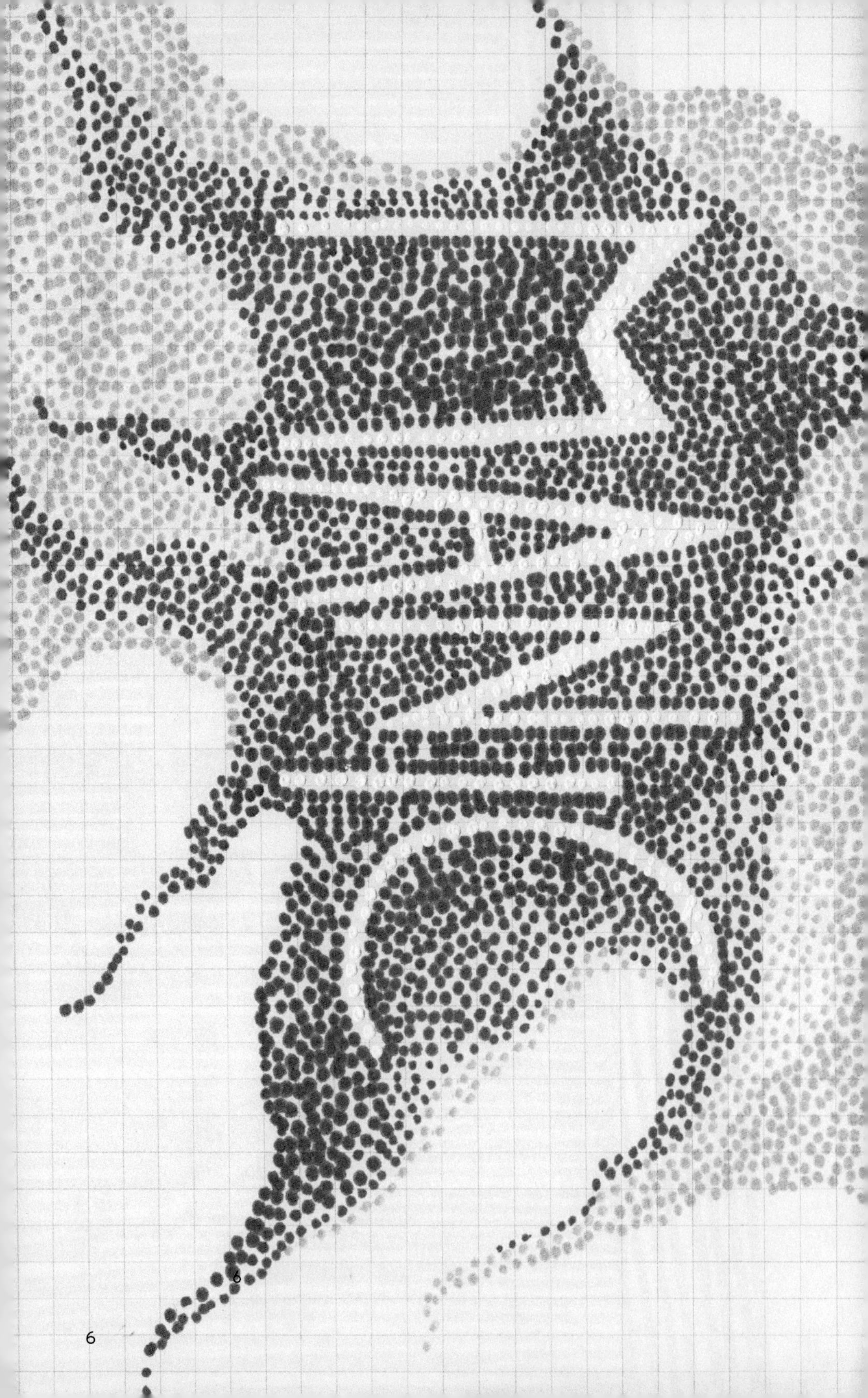

Materials

I keep a metal box with a variety of book making materials in it, such as thread, ribbon, a bone folder, glue, a mechanical pencil, sharpies and a variety of other stuff that comes in handy when I'm stuck for ideas or inspiration. For the projects I have in mind the following things will come in handy:

- Paper. Magazines, newspapers, flyers, and construction paper. Origami paper is a good source of patterns. Tracing paper is awesome for layering, or clear acetate sheets to trace the view from your window.
- Scissors.
- Glue sticks. I like UHU. It's archival which means a year from now your pages won't be brown like with rubber cement and they are safe to use on photographs.
- Pens. Microns are great because they are cheap and come in a variety of sizes. Ball point pens are also good for variety of line weight.
- Markers, sharpies or highlighters. Anything that is colorful.
- A camera and a printer. A phone and your school or office black and white printer are a quick fix.
- Photographs. They can be from your childhood, of your friends, a cat, the sky, anything that interests you.
- A few potatoes to make stamps! Its a cheap, easy way to create patterns.
- Paints and brushes. Acrylics or even cheap watercolors will do nicely.
- Your favorite 3D object.
- Plastic dividers to make stencils.
- Unconventional materials. Nail polish, coffee, or tea are just a few alternatives to markers and paints.
- Needle and thread.
- Linoleum block and carving tools. You can find these at your local art store or online.

THE
PROJECTS

The first section of this book will show a variety of different techniques that can be used in your sketchbook. They start off simple and get more difficult as you get more comfortable with the materials.

The projects are intended to be done over the course of 20 days. If you particularly enjoy a new medium, feel free spend more time on it. The goal of this book is to help you find your style and to push you beyond normal sketchbook conventions.

The restrictions are meant to push you creatively, to be done over the course of a day. If you are feeling uninspired by the project, make something in line with what the project calls for. Forcing yourself to working on your sketchbook every day is a valuable tool to self expression and creativity.

Start looking at your sketchbook as a blank canvas and not just a place to doodle and write. Sketchbooks can be anything you want them to be.

Most importantly, have fun!

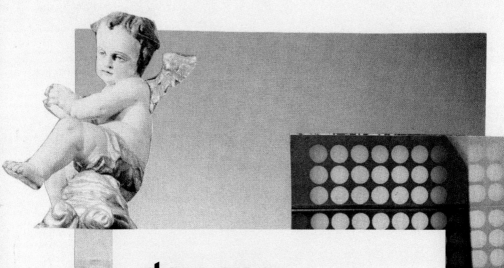

day one:
collage

Using images found in magazines, newspapers, old calendars, or photos, create collages that are visually stimulating to you. The point is to start looking for and collecting cool images and ideas all the time for you sketchbook.

Need some ideas?
Get one of those celebrity weekly magazines, cut out all of the heads and make a pattern.

Try making a fashion mood board of what you'd like to swear next summer.

day two:
text collage

Today, instead of using images, only use text
or letters. Use type found in magazines, newspapers, flyers, anything goes. Focus on the letter
forms, what about them is interesting to you?

Having some trouble?
Write a poem out of different words you find, like
magnetic poetry.

Collect all of the blue letters you can for a couple
of days and create a pattern.

Im sitting outside on this beautiful day.
I was reading a short NASA update or photo
blurb rather and it said how there was a
massive solar flare in September of last year.
The photo showed the sun + flare in comparison
to the earth. As I was reading it the wind
picked up and it was kind of terrifying for a
moment, like the sun was about to swallow
     me up in that instance. I woke up early
(for me) and ate the lunch I made for R.
that he left. Did a bunch around the house.
    That boy will never fold laundry. Cleaned
up the living room, trying to work and wat-
    ching space documentaries. I wonder
         why R. took I. to G.'s moms instead
of having me watch her like he normally does.
He seemed to have decided last night but
    its been quiet around here today. We're
going to foxwoods on Saturday. I'm wondering
    how we're going to get there and if we'll all
get along. My stomach hurts even though I've eaten,
and generally I feel like I'm falling apart. I
    upade updated M. on how my weekend
was, she seemed concerned but is happy
    that I'm ok. Bless her for being here for

ne lately.
at everyo
are for th
s tough no
ost anxi<
minutes s
per awar<

day three:
freewriting

Spend a minimum of ten minutes today writing. This
can be difficult if you're not used to it. If you can't
think of anything to write, start with "I can't think of
anything" and just keep writing. I promise, your
mind will think of something. The point is not to
stop, to let your mind wander and have your hand
be an extension of your thoughts.

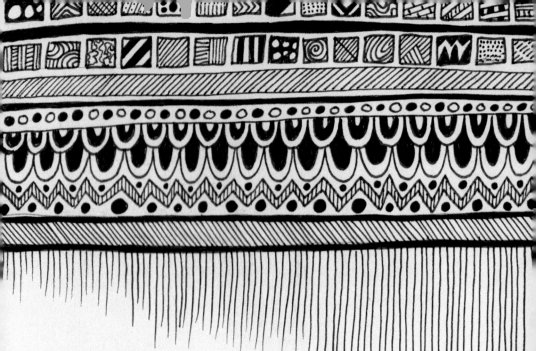

day four:
patterns

Patterns are great for when you aren't feeling very inspired or just want to doodle. Spend today drawing as many patterns as you can. It's a great way to pass the time on the phone or while you're watching TV.

"IT FORCED ME TO
SIT MYSELF DOWN
& DO SOMETHING
   CREATIVE [BECAUSE]
ITS DIFFICULT
   TO FIT CREATIVITY
      INTO MY
   SCHEDULE..."

@ASTRODUB
ON THE BENEFITS
OF HAVING
A DEADLINE

day five:
one color

Collect all of the materials you can in a single color.
Don't be limited to markers. Ads in magazines are
a great way to find loud colors and crazy patterns.
Paints, pencils, even nail polish can add a different
hue to what you might find in a marker. Make
anything you like, but avoid black for starters.

Having some trouble?
Add another color for contrast.

is to represent ideas or con

r the original pictoral form

ame symbols for spoken la

od of the heavens

d (evolved) because the

had an increasing n

sciously sought

developed

numeric

day six: painting

Use paints and brushes in any way that appeals to you. Drip, layer or paint. Experiment with different inks and brushes to figure out your favorite effects.

Having some trouble?
Try dripping paint on one side and closing the book for a Rorschach effect.

If you don't mind getting your hands dirty, try scraping your nails through the bristles of the brush to spray the paint onto the pages.

day seven:
handlettering

Find quotes you like, or individual words and draw it the way you would an illustration. Spend time on every letter. Work bigger to give you lots of space to make patterns.

I like to use hand lettering when I am feeling mean. I'll think "you're a terrible person, but its OK, cos your hair looks great." Instead of insulting someone, I spend 20 minutes drawing it in my book. By the time I'm done I feel a thousand times better and have created something positive out of a negative thought.

24

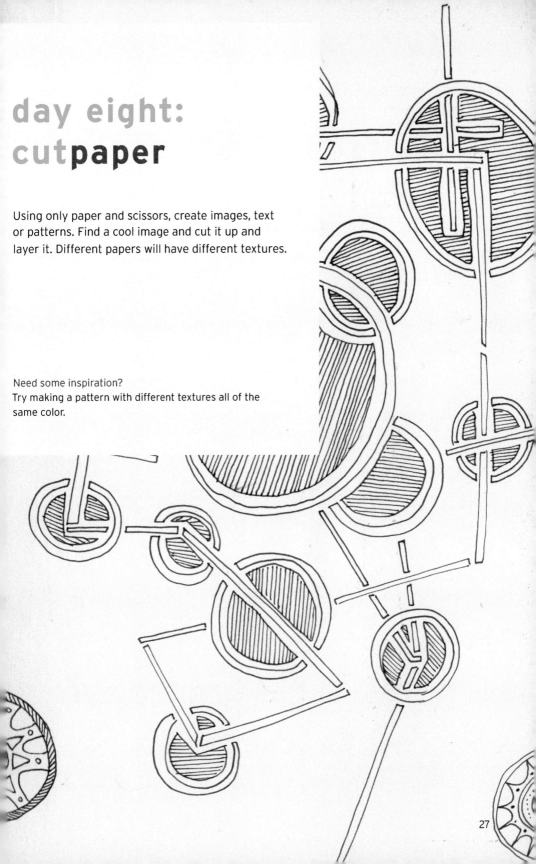

day eight:
cutpaper

Using only paper and scissors, create images, text or patterns. Find a cool image and cut it up and layer it. Different papers will have different textures.

Need some inspiration?
Try making a pattern with different textures all of the same color.

~~10 YEA~~

"MAK
ANY

ole in the week after it was offloaded—the two men were driving back from
li authori- ...ing in the nearby town of V...razi... Calimero wa... surpri...
ah. There, ...bout bureaucratic stuff. But this wa... no routine matter
n July 9 it
of Italy's
shuffli...
year...
rans...
wit...
ne s...
fo...
"hei...
"
...pia T...
...ises
Scot...
...arly
a laptop
Thailand,
d, a water

x

...Mon... quie... t... hem about ... adings, and Ca...
fluence of ...Ga... no hea... he port, sto...ing at their office...
on to ille- ...their ... gear, ...ed radiatio... ...ectors packed...
t of entry ...alu...m case... arrived at ... less than an ho... ...e...

— || —

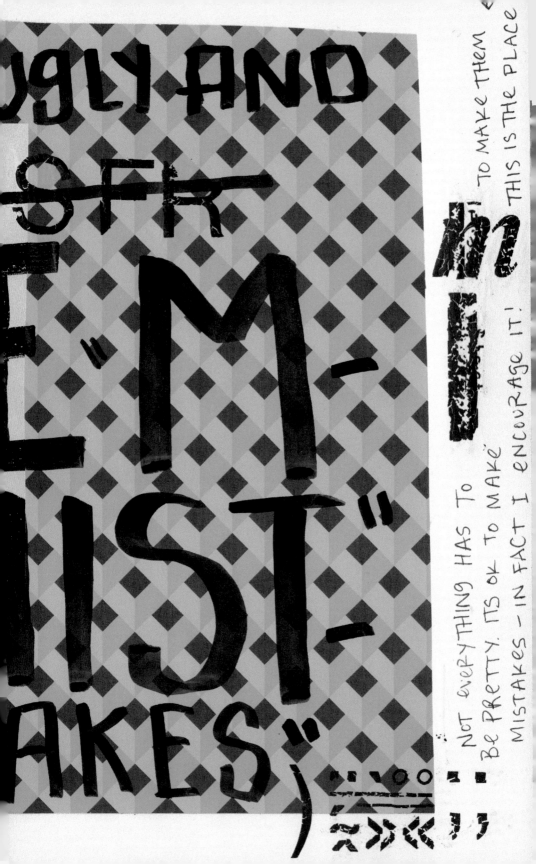

day nine:
found
materials

Receipts, band flyers, old missing cat posters.
When you're out and about, keep your eye out for
bright colors or cool typography. Try not to limit
yourself to just what you can find around the house.
Try painting with coffee, tea or blackberry juice. Use
a feather, fork or lemon instead of a paintbrush.

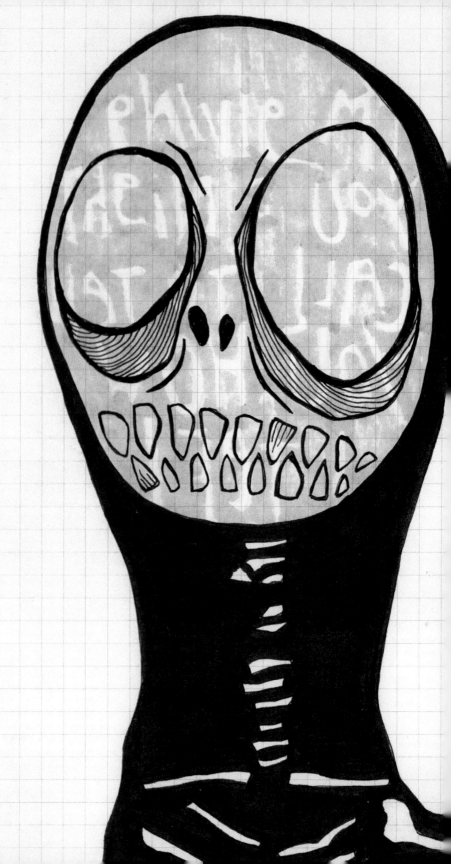

day ten:
characters

Characters are always a lot of fun to draw. If you feel like you're not good at drawing people, try drawing monsters, animals or objects with lots of personality.

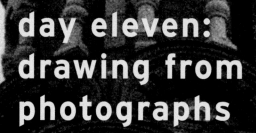

day eleven: drawing from photographs

Spend a day taking pictures of anything that looks even remotely interesting.

Pick your three favorites and print them out. Glue the photo to the left side your sketchbook. Redraw it on the right side.

This is often times easier to do than drawing from observation because a 3D object has been reduced to a 2D field. It is meant as an exercise and to help you practice.

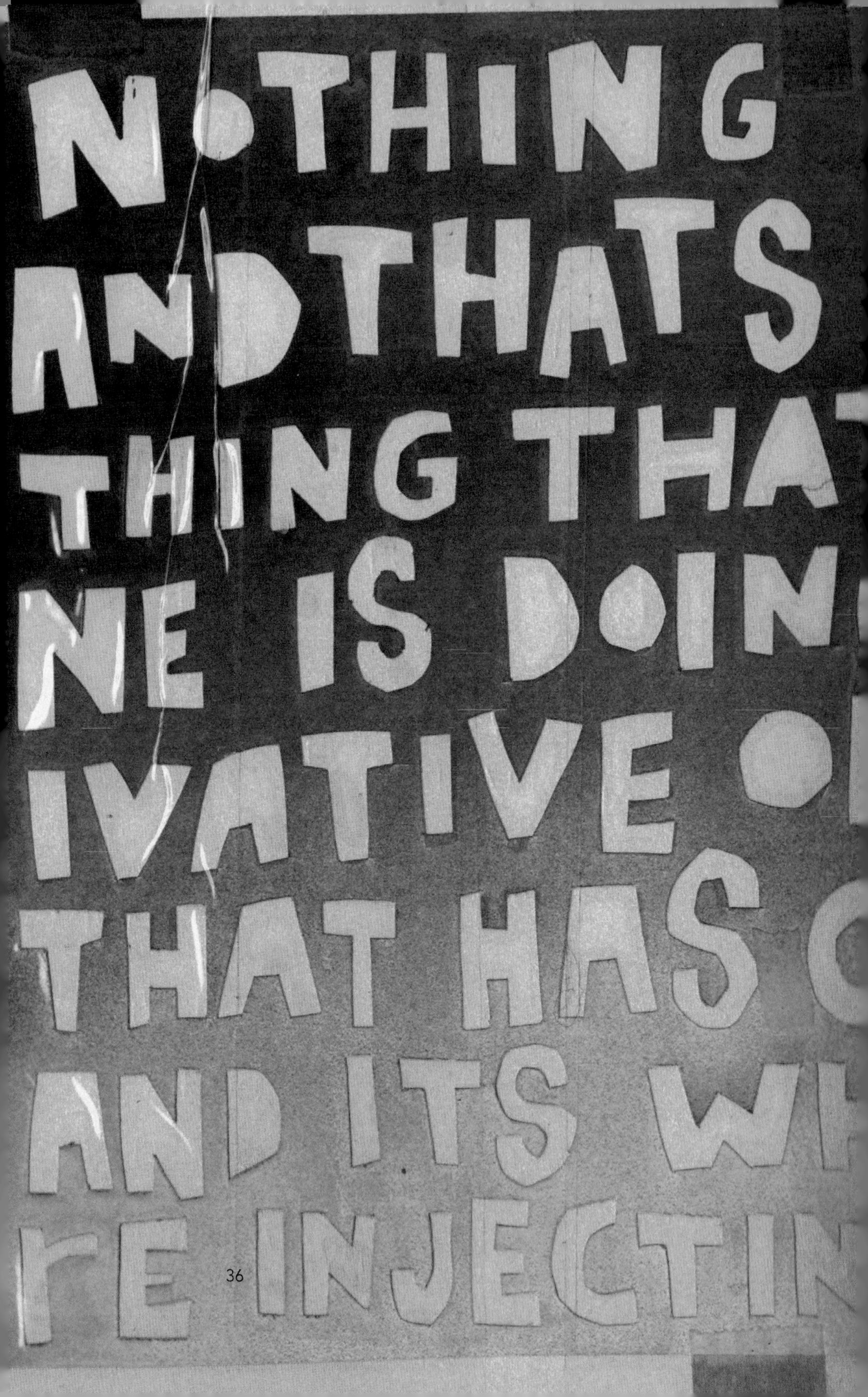

NOTHING
AND THATS
THING THAT
NE IS DOIN
IVATIVE O
THAT HAS O
AND ITS WH
RE INJECTIN

S ORIGINAL
K. EVERY-
EVERYO.
IS A DER-
SOMETHING
OME BEFORE
ETHER YOU'
YOU INTO IT.
@ART IS DEAD ON BEING AN ARIST

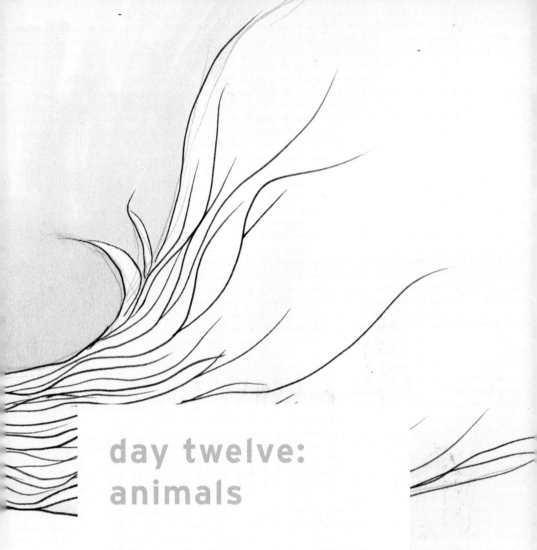

day twelve: animals

Whether or not you have any pets, spend the day drawing animals. You can draw them from observation, photographs, old paintings or imagination.

Need some inspiration?
What will a house cat look like a million years from now?

day thirteen:
potato prints

One way to create dynamic patterns of color in your
sketchbook is to use a potato or an eraser. While
the potato won't last more than a day or two,
it is easy to work with and will have a larger surface
area. Start simple and work your way to more
complex shapes.

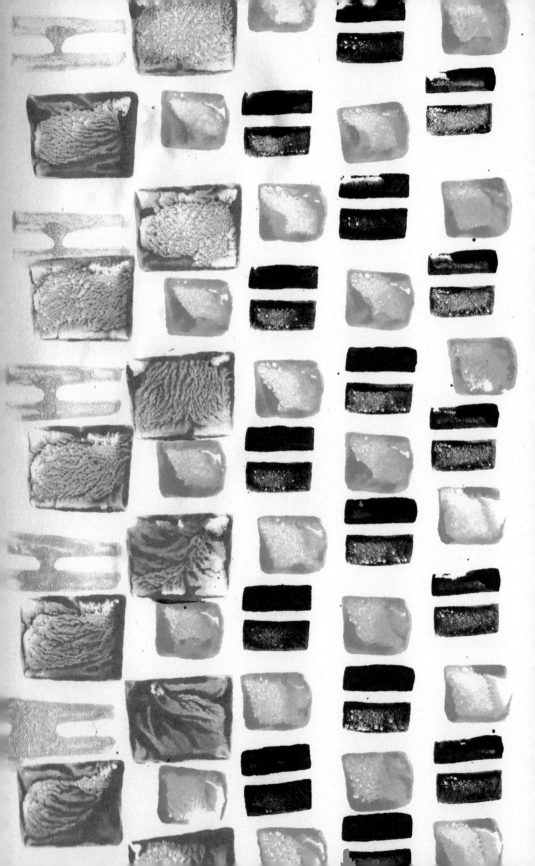

day fourteen:
stippling

Use different width markers and pens to create
images with tiny dot marks. Use layers of different
colors for different effects. Try to avoid using lines
at first to get the feel of it. If you use pencil as an
outline, make sure that the pen or marker you're
using will allow the lines to erase cleanly.

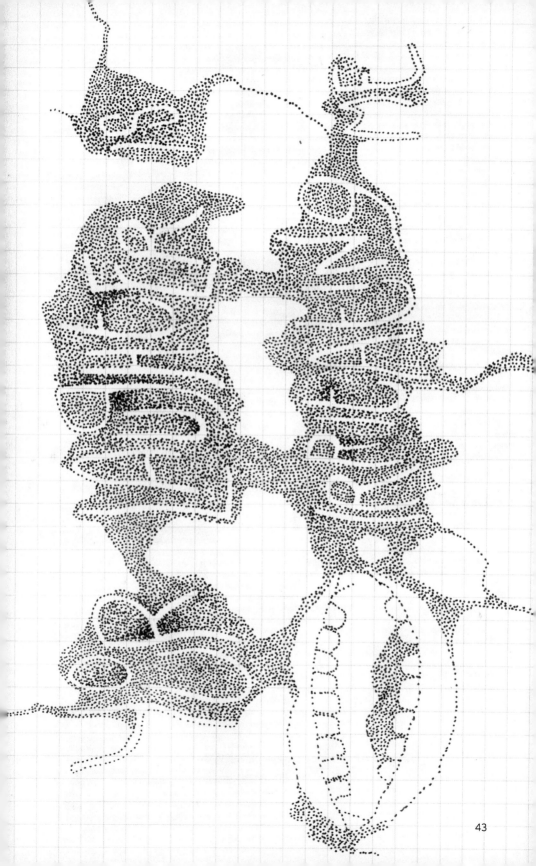

day fifteen: object

Pick an object you like. Set it in front of you and
try to draw it with as much detail as you can.
Try a different angle, lighting and distance from
you. Use different materials, one in pen, one
in paint and one in cut paper for instance.

Need some help?
Jewelry, a crumpled sweater or a bunch of feathers
will all have interesting textures.

Find something that won't get boring too quickly.

BONJOUR

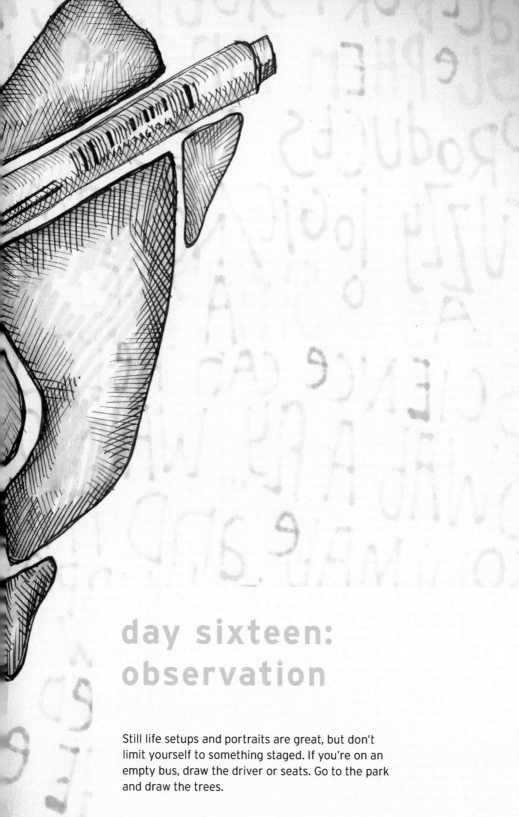

day sixteen:
observation

Still life setups and portraits are great, but don't limit yourself to something staged. If you're on an empty bus, draw the driver or seats. Go to the park and draw the trees.

day seventeen: portraits

Drawing people can be daunting, so start with someone who doesn't know you're drawing them, such as someone in a cafe, reading a newspaper, or someone on tv. It's okay if your drawing doesn't look like the person, the more you practice the easier it will become and you will start to develop a style.

Need some help?
Try drawing ten people in ten minutes, using quick lines to outline the face and body.

day eighteen: stencils

Cut images or words out of plastic divider sheets. Cardboard is fine, but avoid paper, it won't hold up to paint. Tape it to the page and use spray paint or foam brush to apply to your sketchbook.

Need some help?
If you have access Photoshop you can use it to help prepare images.

AND ITS RUBBISH ... beCAUSE IT DOESN'T HAVE AN ENJIN

THIS IS A KAYAK

— THE HAMPST

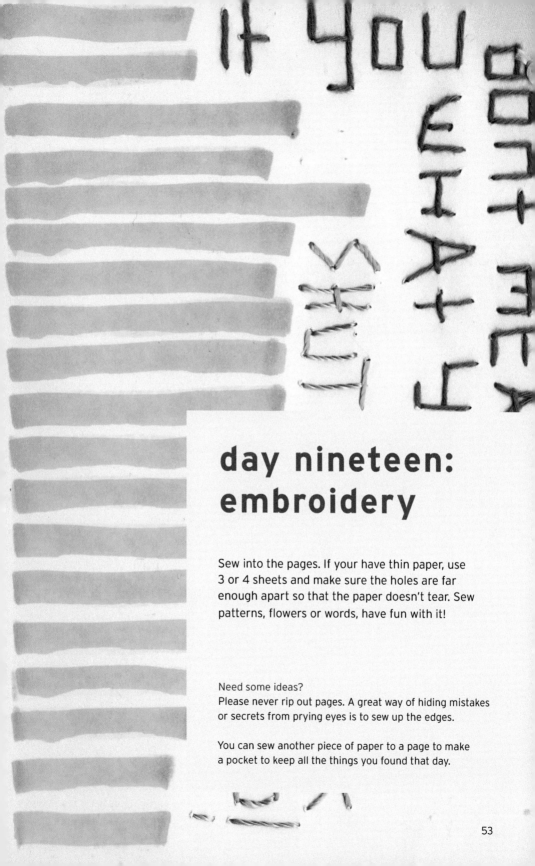

if you dont mea EHAty mux Lou Flu

day nineteen: embroidery

Sew into the pages. If your have thin paper, use 3 or 4 sheets and make sure the holes are far enough apart so that the paper doesn't tear. Sew patterns, flowers or words, have fun with it!

Need some ideas?
Please never rip out pages. A great way of hiding mistakes or secrets from prying eyes is to sew up the edges.

You can sew another piece of paper to a page to make a pocket to keep all the things you found that day.

AD
U
R
SP
TY
P
B
Co

Ke

day twenty:
lino block printing

Lino block printing is a lot of fun. You will need
a linoleum block, carving tools, printing ink
and a roller. After carving your image, use the roller
to put ink on it and press into your sketchbook.
It's a good idea to distribute the weight so that the
block prints evenly.

Need some help?
Start small until you get the hang of it.

Put the block against something heavy so it doesn't move
around too much.

THE TOPICS

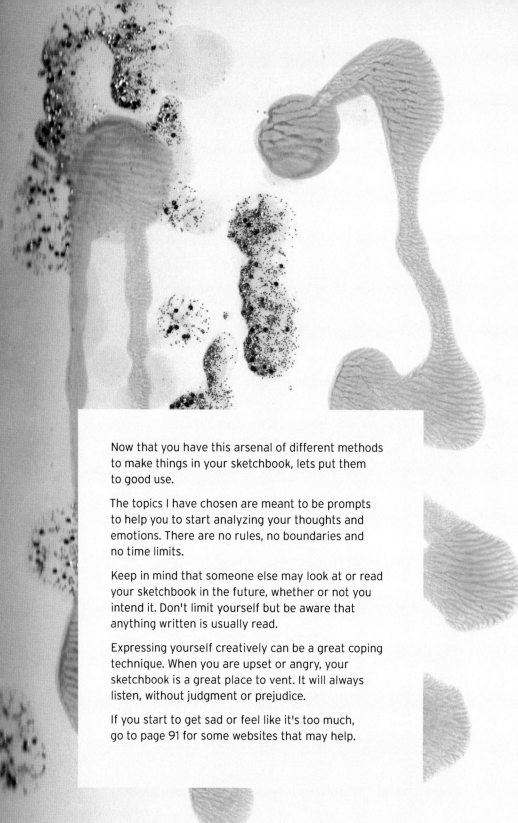

Now that you have this arsenal of different methods to make things in your sketchbook, lets put them to good use.

The topics I have chosen are meant to be prompts to help you to start analyzing your thoughts and emotions. There are no rules, no boundaries and no time limits.

Keep in mind that someone else may look at or read your sketchbook in the future, whether or not you intend it. Don't limit yourself but be aware that anything written is usually read.

Expressing yourself creatively can be a great coping technique. When you are upset or angry, your sketchbook is a great place to vent. It will always listen, without judgment or prejudice.

If you start to get sad or feel like it's too much, go to page 91 for some websites that may help.

"IT WAS VERY
THERAPUTIC TO get
THOSE THOUGHTS OUT,
WHEN YOU HAVE ALL
THAT CRAP ROLLING
AROUND IN YOUR HEAD
IT CAN SNOWBALL.
IT HELPS A LOT TO
get IT OUT OF YOUR
SYSTEM, EVEN IF
ITS NOT VERBALLY,
JUST EXPRESSING YOURSELF.
YOU NEED TO PURGE
YOUR BRAIN."

ANDREW KLASS,
CUT PAPER ATIST,
ON THE BENEFITS
OF KEEPING A
SKETCHBOOK

day twenty one:
friends

Who do you hang out with? Is there anyone you used to know that you miss or don't miss? Who do you think you'll be friends with 10 years from now? What kind of people are they?

day twenty two: family

What kind of family do you have? What are their characteristics? What don't you like about them? What do you love?

Feeling upset?
» When talking about family, sometimes old emotions can surface. If you're feeling upset or overwhelmed turn to the resources on page 91.

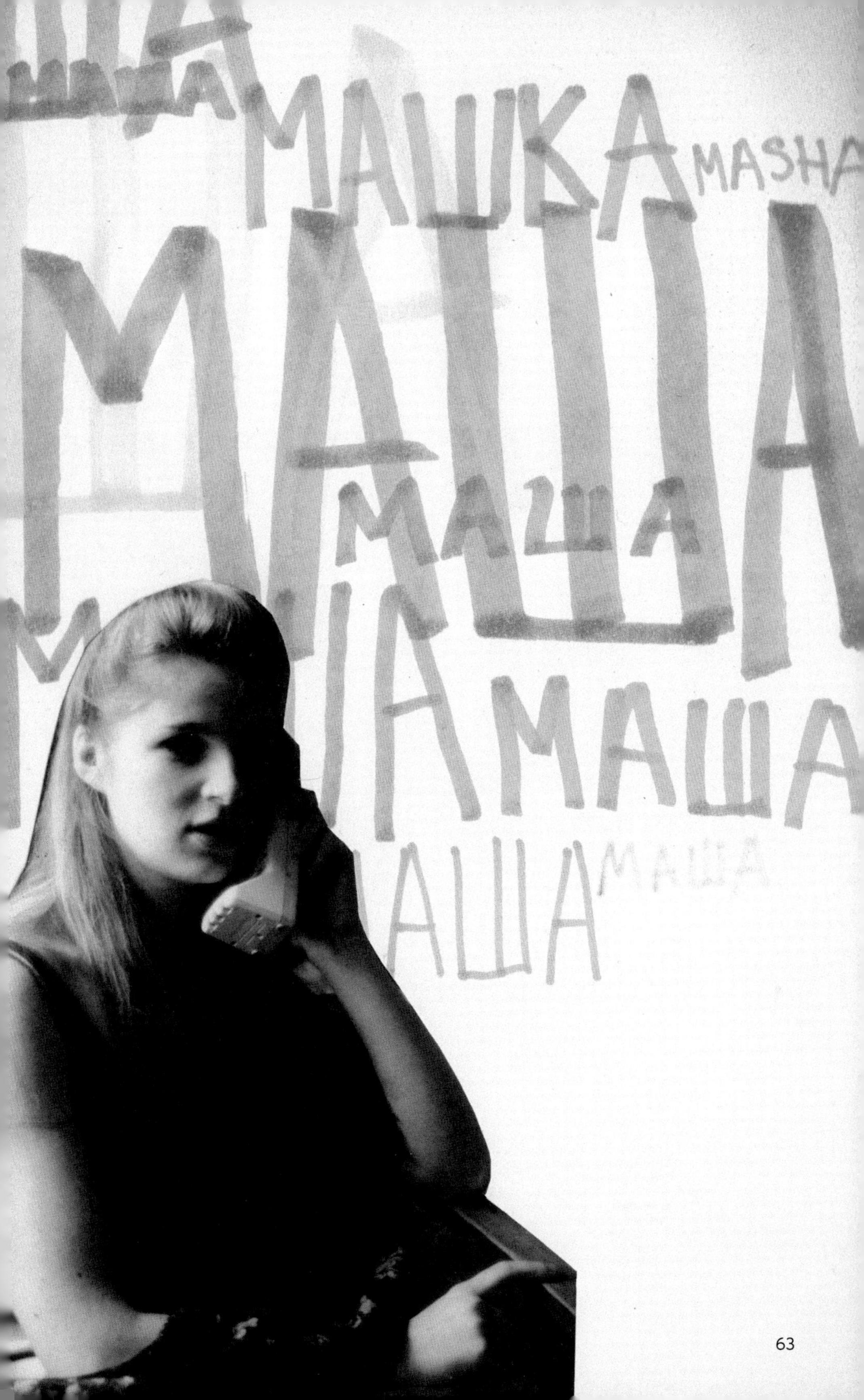

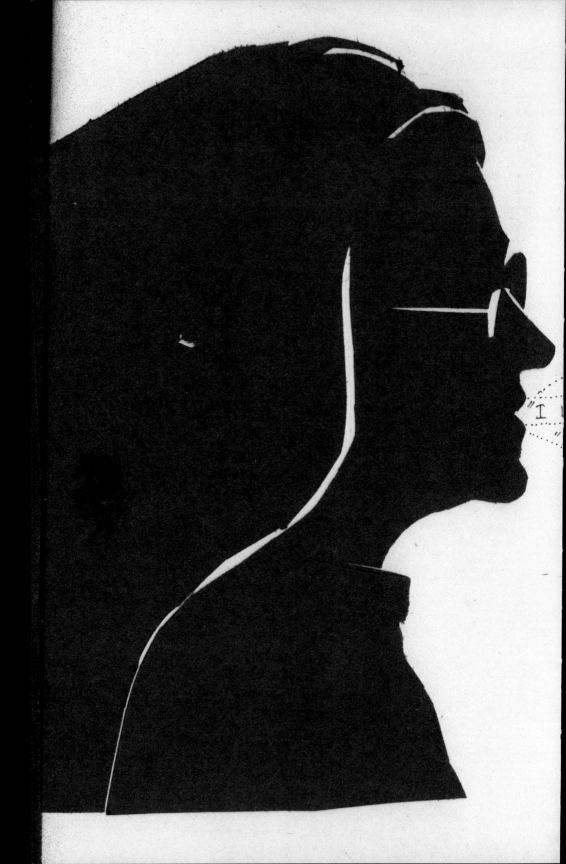

MOTHER

NAME: Galina

Age: 60 - when she turned sixty
she said how she's outlived
her mother by eight years.

Profession: Artist (Eccentric Rambler)

Characteristics: White hair + white glasses

...ler WAS A COUCH"

"INSTAGRAM LOOKS DIFFERENT AGAIN"

...UR PROFILE, LIZA, AND YOUR POINTY NOSE"

"IT WILL BE OKAY. OR NOT. IN WHICH CASE IT WILL BE INFINATELY WORSE"

..."SLUT NURSE OF THE FOREST"

...NTS ARE NOT FLATTERING, BUT THE TOP IS GREAT

BAD HABITS: walking around the
house naked

GOOD HABITS: Reads a lot

day twenty three: dreams

Do you have pleasant or recurring dreams, night-mares, dreams for the future? Draw the people you saw, or write about it. If you don't remember your dreams, what would you like to dream about?

LAST NIGHT I DREMPT THAT MY SUPERHERO FRIENDS AND I HAD A MISSION + AFTER, FOUND OURSELVES FLOATING

IN THE HIGH ATMOSPHERE OF SOME STRANGE PLANET

WE FELL INTO AN OCEAN + I HAD TO RESCUE R2

COS HIS JET BOOSTER

THING WAS BROKEN.

... YEA...

HELP!

THE CLASH

MY WORST FEAR IS TO

their brutally uncompromising music. *The Clash*, the quartet's 1977 debut, remains one of the most vivid documents of the punk era. It became the best-selling import album of the '70s, moving 100,000 copies in the U.S. before "notoriously altered version was released in *don Calling* which spawned its first American hit, "Train in Vain," and led to the eclectic experimentation of 1980's ambitious but bloated triple *Sandinista!*

The Clash imploded in '86, leaving Strummer, in the words of critic Robert Christgau, "a man without a context." (The group was due to reunite in March for their Rock and Roll Hall of Fame induction.) Strummer's post–Clash work—his last album with his band, the Mescaleros, was 2001's *Global a Go-Go*—felt anticlimactic almost by definition. He had embodied

OR THIS

DIE

ALONE

AGAIN

like a warped cosmic jest to learn that Joe Strummer died Dec. 22 of a

likened the Clash's casbah-rocking sound to "a mad seal barking over a mass

day twenty four:
fears

Confronting your fears is a great way to get over
them. What are you afraid of? Whether its spiders
or being lost at sea, your sketchbook is a great
place to vent your fears.

A SKETCHBOOK FOR UNEDITY SOMEWHA AS CAN EXIST THEIR BEAUTY SHOULD ED OUT

I love to ~~dress up and dance!~~

COLOR WITH IZZY

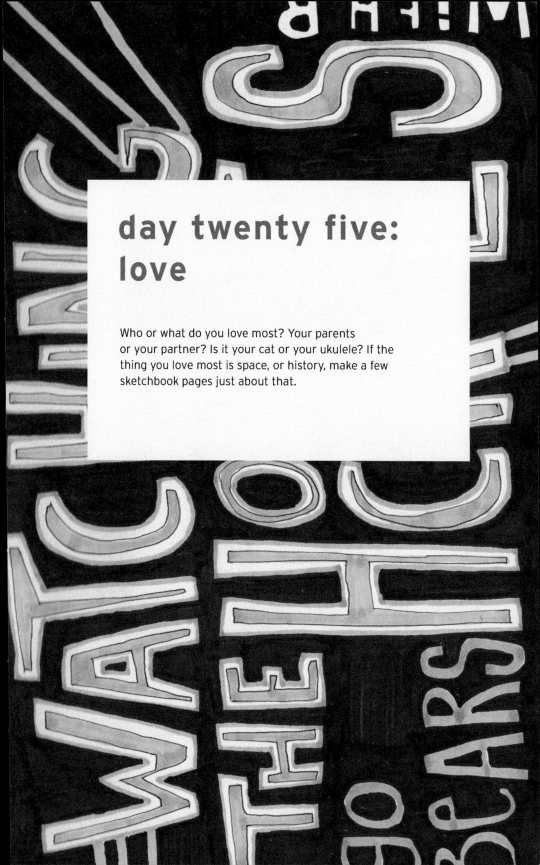

day twenty five: love

Who or what do you love most? Your parents or your partner? Is it your cat or your ukulele? If the thing you love most is space, or history, make a few sketchbook pages just about that.

Date _June 23_ 19 _81_

M _Bless Mom_

No.

Reg. No. _____ Clerk _____ | ACCOUNT FORWARDED

1				
2	2 Dec o legs		90	
3				
4				
5	Paid			
6				
7				
8				
9				
10				
11				
12				
13				
14			4	50
15	44		94	50

Your account stated to date. If error is found, return at once.

WHEN I FIND OLD THINGS
IN OLD BOOKS ITS LIKE CHRISTMAS.
WHO WAS THIS PERSON...
WHAT DID THEY THINK OF THIS BOOK...
IF I COULD TALK TO THEM
WHAT WOULD THEY TELL ME?

day twenty six:
the past

Whats happened to you in your life that has made
you who you are today. What do you think it would
have been like to live 100 years ago? What fascinates you about the distant past? What fascinates
you about your own life so far?

O PLAY MAKES LIZA TIRED AND HUNGRY ALL THE TIM
AND NO PLAY MAKES LIZA A MESS ALL SCHOOL AND
AND NO PLAY MAKES LIZA TIRED ALL SCHOOL AND NO PLA
AND LOST ALL SCHOOL AND ALL CLASS ALL THE TIME
ZA FEEL TIRED ALL THE TIME ALL SCHOOL AND NO PLAY MA
ES LIZA NOD OFF AND STOP PAYING ATTENTION IN CLASS
DIATOR WOULD STOP TURNING ON AND OFF LIFE THAT AL
CHOOL AND NO PLAY MAKES LIZA CRANKY ALL SCHOOL AND
AND NO PLAY MAKES LIZA WISH SHE WAS ON VACATION ALL SCHOOL
NO PLAY MAKES LIZA HUNGRY ALL SCHOOL AND NO PLAY
ES LIZA TIRED ALL SCHOOL AND NO PLAY MAKES LIZA TIRED
MAKES LIZA WANT TO GO HOME ALL SCHOOL AND NO PLAY MAK
CHOOL AND NO PLAY MAKES LIZA TIRED ALL SCHOOL AND NO
O VERY HUNGRY ALL WORK AND NO PLAY MAKES LIZA WIS
J TO GO HOME ALL SCHOOL AND NO PLAY MAKES LIZA SUPER
MA CHE GROWL REALLY LOUDLY IN CLASS ALL WORK AND NO PLA
HOOL AND NO PLAY MAKES ME NOT WANT TO BE IN CLASS RIG
CHOOL WILL BE WORTH THE EFFORT ALL SCHOOL AND NO PL
HEN I HAVE AN AWESOME JOB ALL SCHOOL AND NO PLAY M
ES LIZA SUPER TIRED ALL THE TIME ALL SCHOOL AND NO
O PLAY MAKE ME NOT CARE ABOUT MUCH OF ANYTHING ALL SC
AND NO PLAY MAKES LIZA VERY ANXIOUS ALL SCHOOL AND M
AS HAME ALL SCHOOL AND NO PLAY MAKES LIZA VE
ES LIZA WISH FOR A VACATION ALL SCHOOL AND ALL
LL SCHOOL AND NO PLAY MAKES LIZA WANT TO G
ND CRANKY ALL SCHOOL AND NO PLAY MAKES LI
FIT ALL SCHOOL AND NO PLAY MAKES LIZA T
AKES LIZA TIRED ALL SCHOOL AND NO PLA
PLAY MAKES LIZA WANT TO CRY SOME TIMES
LOONY ALL SCHOOL AND NO PLAY SUCKS ALL
JD NO PLAY IS NO WAY TO LIVE ALL SCHOOL AND NO
OL AND NO PLAY MAKES LIZA WANT TO TAKE A WALK
TIRED AND CRANKY ALL SCHOOL AND NO PLAY M
PLAY MAKES ME TIRED AND CRANKY AND SNAP A
RED ALL SCHOOL AND NO PLAY MAKES LIZA A D

day twenty seven: the present

What is important to you right now? What school do you go to? Who do you hang out with in your grade? What did you do today? Try to stay in the moment and whats happening to you right now.

Not feeling inspired?
Save notes, receipts or any photos your might have taken today and make a collage.

TEN YEARS FROM NOW I WILL BE A SUC-CESSFUL

year gave Boston a brief reason to smile again. / GETTY IMAGE

ARTS   MUSIC   EVENTS   LIFE

day twenty eight: the furute

Where will you be in 10 years? When you graduate high school where would you like to live? What kind of career interests you? If you would like to go to college, what would you like to study?

"MY SKETC

henchman — NO.

or ill conceived

or executio, M

ALWAYS AP

ME to contiue t

wherever it

costant al

war againste

—DOMINIC DEL TO

ILLUSTRATOR

82

book is like an approving matter how stupid

idea, sentiment

sketchbook

loves & allows

journey...

eads. it is a

in my

ness. London

NEVER-ENDING & LOGIC. based

ORIGINALLY PUBLISHED IN SKETCHBOOKS BY RICHARD BRERETON

I LOVE MY GLASSES BUT MY ARM IS WEIRD. I WISH I HADN'T CUT MY HAIR.

I SHOULD USE MY INSTAX MORE. APR. 25

Note to self: BUY BATTERIES.

day twenty nine:
self image

How do you see yourself? Look in the mirror, draw
your face, your hair, your clothes. Draw what
you think is interesting or unique about you. What
do you care about? What are you interested in?
How do others see you? If you're not sure, ask! What
is your moms favorite characteristic of yours or your
best friend? Ask someone to describe you in one
word, three or five.

hype hype h
hype hype
hype hype
hype hype
hyPER!

happy

EXCITED REST

CONTENT

TODAY I feel

EMOT

e L
a t
e D

PEACE

Lovely

day thirty:
emotions

Try to identify what you are feeling. Are you sad or
depressed? Anxious? Angry? Your sketchbook
is a great place to vent. When you're happy, what
is it thats making you so happy? Put it on paper
for next time you're feeling sad.

Feeling upset?
If you're particularly upset and don't know where to turn,
a Suicide Prevention hot line can help. The staff are
every day people that volunteer in order to help people
in a crisis.

Conclusion

Now that you have completed *Empathetic Sketchbook*, the next step is to get a new one and keep working. Keep experimenting, problem solving and discovering yourself. A sketchbook is a tool. It can be anything you want it to be, but its up to you to fill it up.

Have fun, make mistakes and keep creating.

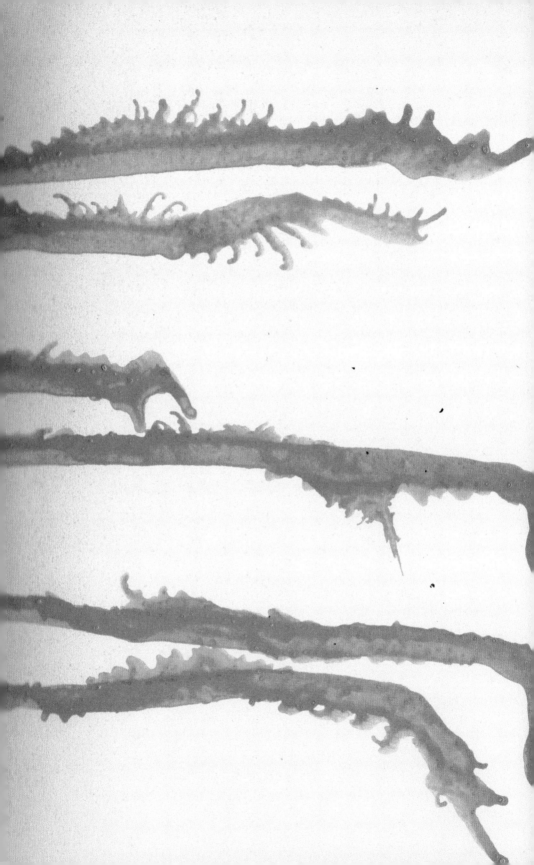

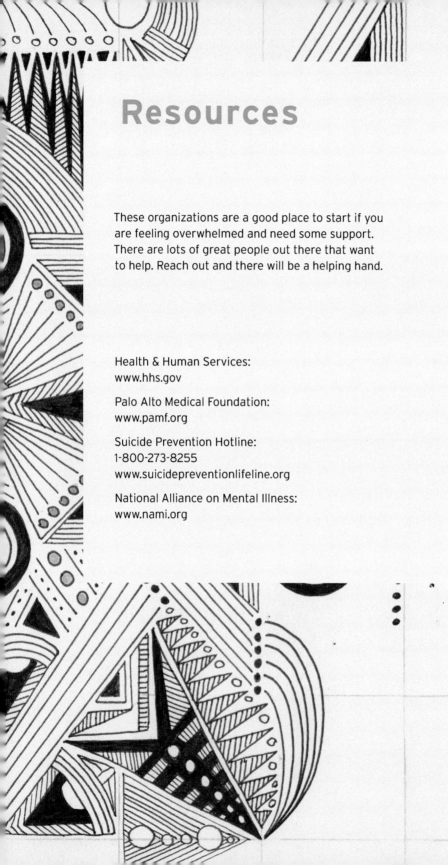

Resources

These organizations are a good place to start if you are feeling overwhelmed and need some support. There are lots of great people out there that want to help. Reach out and there will be a helping hand.

Health & Human Services:
www.hhs.gov

Palo Alto Medical Foundation:
www.pamf.org

Suicide Prevention Hotline:
1-800-273-8255
www.suicidepreventionlifeline.org

National Alliance on Mental Illness:
www.nami.org

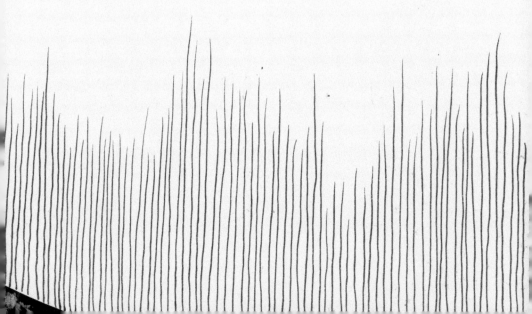

Many thanks

This book would not have been possible without the help and support of many people.

Thanks to MassArt for helping me expand my creative knowledge. @andrewklass, @artisdeaad_76 and @astrodub for contributing to my research. Thanks to Courtney McGlynn for being proud of me and Rob and Izzy for loving me no matter what.

Finally, all my love to Galina Rein for always encouraging me to be creative.

Made in the USA
Coppell, TX
12 January 2020